A Teacher's Guide to

Nature's Food Chains

LESSON PLANS TO TEACH NATURE'S FOOD CHAINS

Using the book *Pass the Energy, Please!* by Barbara Shaw McKinney

By Carol Malnor

In addition to classroom teaching in four states, Carol Malnor has developed educational programs for zoos, high school drop-outs, and a jail. She and her husband Bruce (co-author with her for some of this series of teacher's guides) have conducted teacher training workshops throughout the U.S. and overseas, and distance learning programs on the internet. Currently, Carol is an instructional designer for Performance Learning Systems and editor of *The Heart of Teaching*, a nationwide newsletter for K-12 teachers.

SHARING NATURE
WITH CHILDREN SERIES

Table of Contents

Letter to Teachers 3

Introduction: The Whys & Hows of—
    Multiple Intelligences 4
    Benchmark Standards 5
    Skills for Living 5
    Center Approach to Learning 6

Lesson Plan
    Introduction to *Pass the Energy, Please!* 8

Multiple Intelligences Centers
    Owl Pellets *(Naturalist)* 11
    A Seedy Activity *(Naturalist)* 14
    Eye Witness *(Intrapersonal)* 16
    Animal Interview *(Intrapersonal)* 19
    Dinners and Diners *(Bodily-Kinesthetic)* 22
    Create a Food Chain *(Interpersonal)* 24
    Sounds Good *(Musical-Rhythmic)* 26
    Animal Cinquains *(Verbal-Linguistic)* 28
    Paper Chains *(Visual-Spatial)* 31
    Pyramid Power *(Visual-Spatial)* 36
    Weight and See *(Logical-Mathematical)* 38
    Creature Features *(Logical-Mathematical)* 41

Teacher Background Information 44

Multiple Intelligences Subcapacities 46

How to Teach to the Eight Intelligences 47

Resources 48

Dear Teachers,

The interdependence and interconnectedness of all life is evident as we read about food chains in *Pass the Energy, Please!*

*"Each living thing is a link in the chain,
With a purpose that Nature can always explain."*

Just as each link in the food chain has a unique purpose, every child has special gifts to offer to us and to our world. Using the multiple intelligences reminds us as teachers to appreciate and honor students for their wide variety of talents and abilities. As students feel valued for who they are, their hearts and minds become more receptive to learning.

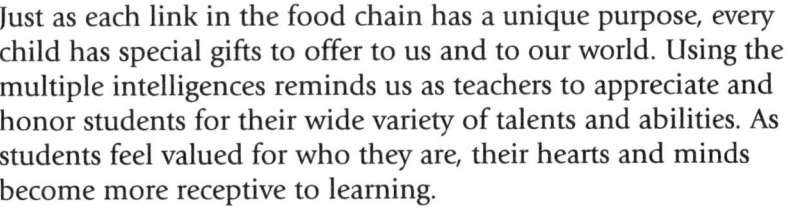

In this teacher's guide there are a dozen different learning centers explained in complete detail. Each center focuses on one of the eight intelligences reinforcing important skills and concepts in science, math, language arts, and life skills. The centers can be used independently, in conjunction with each other, or easily adapted as activities for the entire class to experience together.

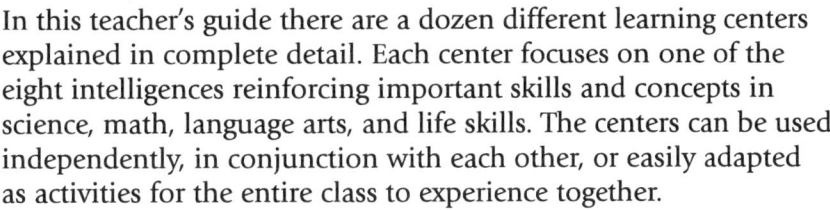

Rachel Carson said, "If children are to keep alive their inborn sense of wonder . . . they need the companionship of at least one adult who can share with them the joy, excitement, and mystery of the world we live in." I invite you to be that adult as you explore the wonders of food chains with your students.

Carol Malnor

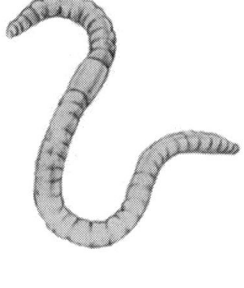

The Whys and Hows

Multiple Intelligences

Why: Multiple intelligences allows us to recognize and work with students and the wide variety of strengths that they bring into the classroom. By encouraging the expression of all of the intelligences, the classroom becomes a place where each individual student feels honored and valued–a place where instructional strategies draw out the highest potential in each student.

The theory of Multiple Intelligences was first introduced by Howard Gardner, a Harvard psychologist. Based on scientific criteria, he has identified eight intelligences.

- Verbal-linguistic intelligence focuses on the use of language and is expressed through reading, writing, and speaking.
- Those with logical-mathematical intelligence can handle long chains of reasoning, recognize problems and like to solve them, and identify patterns.
- Visual-spatial intelligence includes the ability to accurately perceive the visual world, think three-dimensionally, and create mental imagery.
- Musical-rhythmic ability includes discrimination among tone, pitch, rhythm, and timbre, and an awareness of sounds in the environment.
- The bodily-kinesthetic intelligence involves using one's body to learn, communicate, and solve problems, and the capacity to work with objects through either fine or gross motor movements.
- Interpersonal intelligence includes the ability to nurture relationships and friendships, provide leadership, resolve conflicts, and detect the feelings, motives, and concerns of others.
- Intrapersonal intelligence includes the ability to access one's own feelings and emotions and to draw upon them to understand and guide one's own behavior.
- The naturalist ability involves seeing connections, patterns, and relationships among objects or phenomenon in the natural and man-made worlds.

The above list has been compiled from *Purposeful Learning through Multiple Intelligences* by Performance Learning Systems and The New City School. A more extensive listing of the subcapacities for each intelligence can be found on page 46.

How: There are numerous instructional strategies that encourage the development and expression of the eight intelligences. Two of the most important factors in supporting a student's strengths are variety and choice; variety in the way information is presented and learning is communicated, and choice on the part of the students as to how they work with information. A listing of the numerous ways to teach to the different intelligences can be found on page 47.

In this teacher's guide, each center focuses on one of the multiple intelligences. Because the intelligences do not exist in isolation, several intelligences may overlap in an activity; this guide identifies the primary intelligence used by students to achieve the lesson objective.

Benchmarks

Why: Maintaining high standards in the classroom aids student achievement. The benchmarks in *Content Knowledge: A Compendium of Standards and Benchmarks for K-12 Education,* by John S. Kendall and Robert J. Marzano, identify the skills and knowledge which are essential for all students.

How: The suggested unit and lesson plans in this guide identify benchmarks. The Science Benchmarks addressed through this teacher's guide include:

- ❏ Knows that major categories of living organisms are plants, which get their energy directly from sunlight, and animals, which consume energy-rich foods. (Science 4, Level II)
- ❏ Knows that all organisms, including the human species, are part of and depend upon two main global food webs; one global food web starts with microscopic ocean plants and seaweed and includes the animals that feed on them and subsequent animals that feed on the plant-eating animals; the other global food web begins with land plants and includes the animals that feed on them and so forth. (Science 4, Level II)
- ❏ Knows that organisms can be classified according to the function they serve in a food chain — producer, consumer, and/or decomposer of organic matter. (Science 4, Level II)
- ❏ Understands how species depend on one another and on the environment for survival. (Science 7, all Levels)
- ❏ Knows that an organisms' patterns of behavior are related to the nature of that organism's environment, including the kinds and numbers of other organisms present, the availability of food and resources, and the physical characteristics of the environment. (Science 7, Level II)
- ❏ Understands the cycling of matter and flow of energy through the living environment. (Science 8, all Levels)
- ❏ Knows that some source of "energy" is needed for organisms to live and grow. (Science 8, Level II)
- ❏ Knows that all animals depend on plants; some animals eat plants for food while others eat animals that eat the plants. (Science 8. Level II)
- ❏ Knows that over the whole Earth, organisms are growing, dying, and decaying, and new organisms are being produced by the old ones. (Science 8, Level II)
- ❏ Knows that almost all food energy ultimately comes from the Sun as plants convert light into stored chemical energy. (Science 8, Level III)

Skills for Living

Why: One of our goals as teachers is to help our students lead successful lives. True success is measured not only by material standards, but also by the quality of life: happiness, fulfillment, joy. The attitudes and qualities which lead us toward true success are called Skills for Living. Like all skills, they can be taught and practiced. As Emerson said, "Character is more important then intellect." When we help our students develop their character, we are not only helping them, we are also contributing to the future of our planet.

How: Each center focuses on one or more of the Skills for Living including cooperation, respect, concentration, perseverance, orderliness, creativity, introspection, problem-solving, curiosity, and appreciation. Simply doing the activity in the center gives students practice with the skill. It can be helpful for students to have each skill identified by name so that they can understand the skill more completely and apply it in other contexts. In this guide, at least one of the Reflection Questions for each center addresses a Skill for Living. With continued practice and application, students internalize the Skills for Living and make them their own.

Center Approach to Learning

Why: The primary purpose of centers is to provide enrichment and reinforcement of skills and content information by having students work independently. A multiple intelligences approach to learning centers gives all students an opportunity to explore content in ways that comes most easily to them. By rotating through centers, students gain experience in using all of the intelligences. Using centers also gives teachers an opportunity to step into the role of facilitator as they circulate from center to center, answering questions and guiding the learning experiences.

How: Each classroom is unique; the specific way the centers are used will depend on your needs, your students, your classroom environment, and your personal teaching style. The centers described in this teacher's guide are designed to accommodate a wide variety of situations and can easily be adapted to suit your particular situation.

Number of Centers:

I suggest eight centers — one center for each of the identified intelligences. The center may be a table that is permanently set up with the necessary materials or a center can be created when needed by having students move their desks together. There are two center choices for the Visual-Spatial, Logical-Mathematical, Intrapersonal, and Naturalist intelligences. You may want to set up both centers and allow students to choose; or select the one center most appropriate for your students.

Set up:

Each center activity described in this guide lists all of the materials and teacher preparation that is needed. The materials are easily available except for owl pellets that need to be ordered. (See ordering information in the center entitled *Owl Pellets*. Allow one week for delivery.)

Each center has a page of *Center Directions* that is to be copied and placed at the center for students to read. I suggest laminating the directions. Keeping each center's materials in a separate box allows you to set up and put away the center quickly and easily.

In setting up the location for each of your centers, please note that *Creature Features* and *Dinners and Diners* are the two noisiest activities, while *Sounds Good* needs a quiet area. The following centers also require wall space to display finished products: *Animal Interview, Creature Features, Create a Food Chain, Paper Chain Bulletin Board,* and *Pyramid Power Poster.*

Number of students at each center:

Four students at a center is an ideal number. Depending on the size of your class, you can divide the class evenly between the centers or set up fewer centers at a time. *Creature Features* requires that students work in pairs, while *Dinners and Diners* is a cooperative group activity. All of the centers can be adapted for a small group or whole-class activity.

Time allowed:

Although students work at different rates, each center is designed to be completed in about an hour. Centers can be used for an hour a day, one or more hours several times a week, or for an entire afternoon or morning. Center activities are a wonderful way to add variety and interest to your schedule.

Center Rotation:

The centers in this guide can be done in any order. I suggest doing the *Owl Pellets* center as a whole-class activity before doing any of the other centers. Then students can return to *Owl Pellets* if they finish early with any of the other centers. (See Suggested Two-Week Unit below.)

Let students know the rotation you will be using ahead of time so that they are clear about when they will be at each center. A chart on the wall can serve as a helpful reminder for everyone.

Considerations:

Before beginning to use a center approach to learning, it is important for you to consider several factors. How much noise can you comfortably tolerate in your classroom? What behavior do you expect from your students? What are the consequences of off-task behavior? What can your students expect of you? How would you like students to indicate that they need your help? How much room do you have in the classroom to set up centers?

Reflection Questions:

Students learn not from their experiences, but from reflecting upon their experiences. That is why it is crucial to debrief with students when doing center activities. You may ask the Reflection Questions while you are visiting each center, have students discuss the questions among themselves at the end of each center time, or have students do the questions as homework to be turned in the next day.

Assessment:

There is a final product (poster, chart, performance, tape, etc.) for each center in this guide. You may choose to develop rubrics for assessing each product or simply use a complete/incomplete system for assessment.

Suggested Two-Week Unit on Food Chains

Day One:	Introduction to *Pass the Energy, Please!*
Day Two:	Owl Pellets
Day Three through Day Nine:	seven centers
Day Ten:	Wrap up — watch skits, listen to tapes, read cinquains, and review what was learned at the centers.

Lesson Plan:

Introduction to Pass the Energy, Please!

 ### Objective:
Introduce the science Benchmarks in the book *Pass the Energy, Please!*

 ### Benchmarks:
See those listed under the *Whys and Hows* beginning on page 5

 ### Skill for Living: Awareness — looking at the world with greater perception

 ### Materials:
- Variety of chains of different lengths, weight, and thickness such as a necklace chain, a bicycle chain, a tow chain, etc.
- Thirty-two 3x5 cards
- *Pass the Energy, Please! Questions* (Copy Master page 10) — one per student group
- Blackboard or chart paper
- Multiple copies of the book *Pass the Energy, Please!* — one copy per student group

 ### Teacher Preparation:
- Draw a series of chains on the blackboard or chart paper (See Section III of the lesson plan for the length of each of the chains: two individual chain links plus a series of seven chains). Make the links about 3x5 inches in size.
- Write one of the following words on each 3x5 card: green plant, seaweed, stems, gorilla, bamboo, panda, sea of grass, gazelle, cheetah, milkweed seed, mouse, snake, owl, phytoplankton, zooplankton, anchovy, seal, polar bear, goldenrod, caterpillar, spider, warbler, weasel, red fox, vulture, beetle, maggot, moth, ant, bacteria, fungus, earthworm. (Total: 32 cards)
- Tape one card to the bottom of every student chair. Depending on your class size, some students may have more than card.

Section I:
Begin class wearing, carrying, and dragging a wide variety of many different chains. Explain that each piece of the chain is called a "link." Dramatically hold up the chains one at a time and ask students if they can identify their use. Emphasize how each chain is perfectly designed for how it is used. For example, a necklace chain consists of very lightweight links so that it isn't too heavy around your neck when you wear it, and a tow chain is extremely thick and heavy so that it can pull a lot of weight without breaking.

Section II:
Tell students that there is one other type of chain that you want them to know about. Show them the book *Pass the Energy, Please!* and tell them that the book is about food chains. Ask students if they know what a food chain is and take responses. Tell them that taped under their chairs they will find a 3x5 card that identifies a link in a food chain. Explain that you will read aloud a passage from the book about a food chain. They should be listening carefully to see if their "link" is mentioned in the food chain you read about. When you are finished with the passage, ask students to bring their links up to the blackboard or chart and tape them in correct order onto the chain you have drawn. Before beginning to read aloud, check to make sure that all students can read their links, especially phytoplankton and zooplankton. Tell students that their links will be explained during the reading of the book.

Section III:
Read aloud pages 4 and 5 (one link: green plant)

Pages 6 and 7 (one link: seaweed)

Pages 8 and 9 (two links: stems, gorilla)   (two links: bamboo, panda)

Pages 10 and 11 (three links: sea of grass, gazelle, cheetah)

Pages 12 through 15 (four links: milkweed seed, mouse, snake, owl)

Pages 16 through 19 (five links: phytoplankton, zooplankton, anchovy, seal, polar bear)

Pages 20 through 23 (six links: goldenrod, caterpillar, spider, warbler, weasel, red fox)

Pages 24 to 26 (broken chain of decomposers: vulture, beetle, maggot, moth, ant, bacteria, fungus, earthworm)

Section IV:
Divide students into groups of three to five students each and give each group a copy of the book *Pass the Energy, Please!* and a copy of the handout *Pass the Energy, Please! Questions*. Assign specific questions for each group to answer. Then, as a whole class, go over all of the answers. Explain to the class that they will be exploring the topic of food chains and the interdependence of all life through various center activities. (You may choose to explain the Multiple Intelligences Centers at this time or wait for the next class time.)

Pass the Energy, Please! Questions

Directions: Write out the answers to your assigned questions.

1. Where do plants get their energy?

2. Where do animals get their energy?

3. What is an herbivore? Give two examples.

4. What is a carnivore? Give two examples.

5. How is the food chain in the ocean similar to the food chain on land?

6. Why is a goldenrod plant important to an fox?

7. What is at the beginning of every food chain?

8. What happens to organisms that die?

9. How can humans endanger animals and their food chains?

10. Which food chain was the most interesting to you?

Center:

Owl Pellets

Multiple Intelligence: *Naturalist*

Objective: Examine owl pellets for evidence of rodent, vole, shrew, or bird bones.
Classify and identify bones.
Optional: Reconstruct a rodent skeleton

Benchmarks:

Knows that objects can be classified by their physical properties. (Science 10, Level I)

Knows that living things can be sorted into groups in many ways using various properties to decide which things belong to which group; features used for grouping depend on the purpose of the grouping. (Science 4, Level II)

Knows that all animals depend on plants; some animals eat plants for food while others eat animals that eat the plants. (Science 8, Level II)

Knows that all species ultimately depend on one another; interactions between two types of organisms include producer/consumer, predator/prey, parasite/host, and relationships that can be mutually beneficial or competitive. (Science 7, Level III)

Effectively uses mental processes that are based on identifying similarities and differences (compares, contrasts, classifies). (Life Skills: Thinking and Reasoning 3, Levels I, II, and III)

Skill for Living: Concentration — being able to focus attention.

Materials:

Owl Pellets (See description in *Center Directions*.) — one per student or student group
Toothpicks — one per student
Paper plates — two per student
Owl Pellets — Bone Identification Chart (Copy Master page 13) — one per student
Optional: magnifying glasses for students to share
Optional: spray bottle of water—for teacher to use to spray pellets to make them easier to break apart.

Teacher Preparation:

Order owl pellets. They are available from Pellets, Inc., Kim and Bret Gaussoin, PO Box 5484 Bellingham, WA 98227, Phone: 360-733-3012 OR (fax) 360-738-3402, http://www.pelletsinc.com. Allow one week for delivery.
Make copies of *Owl Pellets — Bone Identification Chart*.
Copy and laminate *Center Directions*.

Reflection Questions:

1. What kinds of bones did you find in the pellet?
2. Were the bones difficult to identify and classify?
3. What techniques and strategies did you develop as you took apart the pellet and classified bones? What will you do the same or differently when you work with the pellets next time?
4. What information did the pellets give you about the owl's diet? Is the owl an herbivore or a carnivore? A predator or prey?

Note: Students have a lot of fun with this activity and can get very excited as they find the bones. I suggest that you do this activity first with the whole class, and then set up the materials at a center for students to explore again during center time.

Center Directions:
Owl Pellets

At this center you will:
Take apart owl pellets to discover information about the owl's diet.
Identify and classify the bones you find.

Materials you should find at this center:
Owl Pellets — one per student or student group
Toothpicks — one per student
Paper plates — two per student
Copy of *Owl Pellets —Bone Identification Chart* — one per student

What you need to bring to this center:
Paper and pencil
Concentration — being able to focus attention.

Student Directions:

1. Owl pellets are the compact undigested parts (bones and fur) from an owl's diet. Several hours after a meal, an owl will spit out a pellet. Put the owl pellet on one of your paper plates.

2. Using the toothpick, gently begin pulling it apart. As you separate the pellet you will find tiny bones mixed in with the fur. Wetting the pellet with water can sometimes help to loosen the fur.

3. Put the bones on the other paper plate. Use the *Bone Identification Chart* to identify the bones you find. Sort them by putting them in different parts of the paper plate. For example, the skulls go in one area, the leg bones in another, the ribs in another. You may have one area on your plate for unidentified bones.

4. Once you have sorted all of the bones in your pellet, count how many of each type you found and write the information on your paper. You may use this information at a later time.

5. Keep the bones in a place designated by your teacher. Throw away the toothpicks, paper plates, and fur. **Wash your hands.**

Extension Activities:
Put together a complete skeleton of a rodent.
Graph the amounts of each kind of bone that the class found.

Bone Identification Chart

	Rodents	Shrews	Moles	Birds
Skulls				
Jaws				
Shoulder Blades				
Front Legs				
Hips				
Hind Legs				
Assorted Ribs				
Assorted Vertebrae				

CATERPILLAR LARVAE AND COCOONS

CATERPILLAR DROPPINGS

COPY MASTER

Center: A Seedy Activity

Multiple Intelligence: *Naturalist*

 *Objective:* Categorize seeds using a criterion.

 *Benchmarks:*
Knows that objects can be classified by their physical properties. (Science 10, Level I)

Knows that living things can be sorted into groups in many ways using various properties to decide which things belong to which group; features used for grouping depend on the purpose of the grouping. (Science 4, Level II)

Effectively use mental processes that are based on identifying similarities and differences [compares, contrasts, classifies]. (Life Skills: Thinking and Reasoning 3, Levels I, II, and III)

 *Skill for Living:* Organization — The ability to plan, arrange, and implement in an orderly way.

 *Materials:*
- Assortment of at least 12 varieties of seeds such as squash, corn, bean, marigold, sunflower, carrot, beet, lettuce, pumpkin, pea, cucumber, cosmos, buckwheat, rice, wheat, lentils
- Paper towel — one sheet per student at the center
- Plastic baggies — one per student at the center
- Optional: Pictures (from seed packet) of each of the plants that the seeds will produce mounted on a piece of poster board; tape or glue

 *Teacher Preparation:*
- Put an assortment of twelve different seeds into plastic baggies. The seeds should look different from each other and have different qualities; for example, a large seed, a tiny seed, a vegetable seed, a flower seed, a seed that can be eaten as it is (e.g., pumpkin seed).
- Tear apart sheets of paper towel.
- Copy and laminate *Center Directions*.
- Optional: Tape or glue plant pictures to a piece of poster board. Prepare a "key" of the seeds with their corresponding plants on the back of poster board.

 *Reflection Questions:*
1. Into how many different categories were you able to sort the seeds?
2. What was the most unusual criterion you used?
3. How successful were other students in figuring out the criterion for your categories?
4. How did you decide on the way you organized the seeds?

Center Directions:

Seedy Activity

At this center you will:
> Sort seeds into categories using your own specifications.
> Determine the specifications that someone else used to sort their seeds.

Materials you should find at this center:
> A plastic baggie filled with seeds.
> A sheet of paper towel.
> Optional: A poster board with a picture of each plant that the seeds will produce mounted on a piece of poster board.

What you need to bring to this center:
> Pencil or pen
> Two pieces of paper
> Organization — the ability to plan, arrange, and implement in an orderly way.

Student Directions:

1. Empty a baggie of seeds onto a sheet of paper towel. Look carefully at each seed noticing its size, shape, and color. Identify any seeds that you can. For example, you may easily recognize a pumpkin seed.

2. Sort the seeds into three or more groups based on specifications that you decide. For example, some groups might be "seeds that grow vegetables," "seeds that are oval-shaped," "seeds that are larger than 1/4 inch long." Be creative and look for unusual and unique ways to group your seeds. Write down the names of your seed groupings on one of your pieces of paper.

3. When you are finished, turn the paper over and switch places with another student. Carefully look at their seed groups and guess what specifications they used to group their seeds. On your other piece of paper, write the names of what you think their groupings might be. Turn their paper over to check your answers. Continue until you have looked at everyone's seed groupings.

4. When finished, put the seeds back in the plastic baggie.

> If you have additional time, do one of these activities:
> 1. Look at the pictures of the plants that are grown from the seeds and match the seed to the correct plant.
> 2. Choose one seed and write a detailed description of it. Pair up with one other student, read your description, and ask that student to choose the seed that was described. Switch roles and identify his/her seed.
> 3. Rearrange your seeds to group them in entirely different ways.

Center: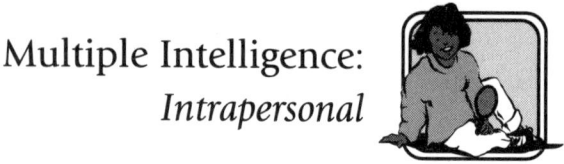

Eye Witness

Multiple Intelligence: *Intrapersonal*

 ### *Objective:*
Identify animals students have seen that are found in the book *Pass the Energy, Please!*. Write about a meaningful experience with an animal.

 ### *Benchmark:*
Demonstrates competence in autobiographical writing. (Language Arts 1, Levels II and III)

 ### *Skill for Living:* Introspection — being able to look within self.

 ### *Materials:*
- *Eye Witness Animal Chart* (Copy Master page 18) — one copy for each student group that uses the Center.
- Envelopes — two
- Small red and blue dot stickers to fit on the *Eye Witness Animal Chart* — one of each per student
- Student journals or paper
- Drawing paper
- Crayons, colored pencils, and/ or markers

 ### *Teacher Preparation:*
- Copy the *Eye Witness Animal Chart*.
- Put red dots in one envelope and blue dots in the other envelope.
- Copy and laminate *Center Directions*.

 ### *Reflection Questions:*
1. Did you use more red dots or blue dots?
2. What animals from the book live in your area?
3. Did you see most of the animals in their natural habitats or at a zoo?
4. Why did you choose to write about the animal that you did?

Center Directions:

Eye Witness

At this center you will:
Put stickers next to the names of animals you have seen or would like to see.
Write about a meaningful time you have had with an animal.

Materials you should find at this center:
Two envelopes containing red and blue dot stickers
Eye Witness Animal Chart
Drawing paper
Crayons, colored pencils, or markers

What you need to bring to this center:
Journal or paper to write on
Pencil or pen
Introspection — being able to look within yourself.

Student Directions:

1. Put a red dot sticker in the "Have Seen" column of the *Eye Witness Animal Chart* next to the name of all of the animals you have seen.

2. Put a blue dot sticker in the "Want to See" column of the *Eye Witness Animal Chart* next to the name of all of the animals you would like to see.

3. Write a description in your journal about a special time you have spent with an animal. The animal might be your pet, a bird that comes to a bird feeder in your backyard, or one of the animals on the chart. Write about why it was a special experience for you.

4. Draw a picture either in your journal or on a piece of drawing paper to illustrate your special experience.

Eye Witness Animal Chart

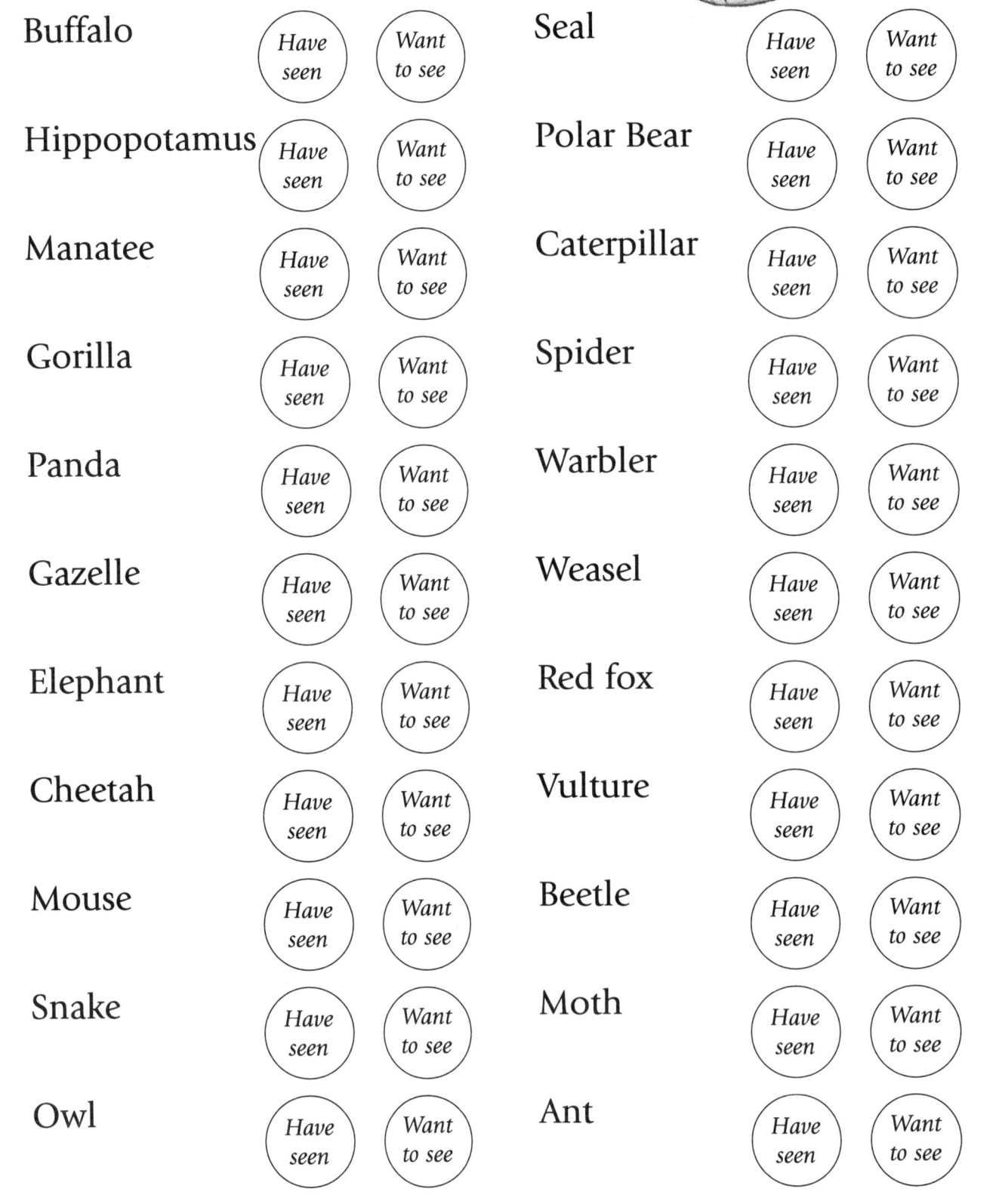

Animal			Animal		
Buffalo	Have seen	Want to see	Seal	Have seen	Want to see
Hippopotamus	Have seen	Want to see	Polar Bear	Have seen	Want to see
Manatee	Have seen	Want to see	Caterpillar	Have seen	Want to see
Gorilla	Have seen	Want to see	Spider	Have seen	Want to see
Panda	Have seen	Want to see	Warbler	Have seen	Want to see
Gazelle	Have seen	Want to see	Weasel	Have seen	Want to see
Elephant	Have seen	Want to see	Red fox	Have seen	Want to see
Cheetah	Have seen	Want to see	Vulture	Have seen	Want to see
Mouse	Have seen	Want to see	Beetle	Have seen	Want to see
Snake	Have seen	Want to see	Moth	Have seen	Want to see
Owl	Have seen	Want to see	Ant	Have seen	Want to see

COPY MASTER

Center:

Animal Interview

Multiple Intelligence: *Intrapersonal*

Objective: Research answers to self-formulated questions about animals.

Benchmarks:
Asks and seeks to answer questions regarding the characteristics of various places outside the local community and those who live in those places. (Language Arts 4, Level II)

Uses encyclopedias and dictionaries to gather information for research topics. (Language Arts 4, Level II)

Independently applies the reading process and strategies to passages about the sciences. (Language Arts 9, Levels II and III)

Skill for Living: Curiosity — having a sense of wonder about the world.

Materials:
- *Animal Interview — I Wonder* (Copy Master page 21) — minimum of one per student (some students may use two or three)
- Wide variety of books, magazines, encyclopedias, videos, and other resources about animals including computer for Internet access and TV and VCR for viewing videotapes.
- Wall space for posting completed *Animal Interview — I Wonder* handouts.

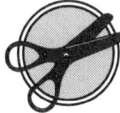
Teacher Preparation:
- Make copies of *Animal Interview — I Wonder* (Copy Master)
- Gather resources.
- Copy and laminate *Center Directions*.

Reflection Questions:
1 Were you able to find answers to most of your questions?
2. What was the most interesting piece of information that you discovered?
3. Did your research lead you to additional questions and answers?
4. What type of resource (book, magazine, video, etc.) was most helpful for you?

Center Directions:

Animal Interview

At this center you will:
Write three questions about an animal of your choice as if you were interviewing that animal. For example, if you chose a bear, you might ask, "How do you hibernate?" " How much do you weigh?" "How dangerous are you to people?" Use the resources at this center to find the answers to your interview questions.

Materials you should find at this center:
Magazines, books, videos, and other resources about animals.
Copies of the handout *Animal Interview — I Wonder*.

What you need to bring to this center:
Pencil or pen
Curiosity — having a sense of wonder about the world.

Student Directions:

1. Write (in the appropriate space of the handout) the name of an animal that you would like to find out more about.

2. Write down three questions you have about the animal. The questions can be about what the animal eats, where it lives, how it raises its young, if it's endangered, etc.

3. Once you have your questions written, begin looking through the resources to find your answers. Write your answers on the handout. Be sure to use correct spelling and write in complete sentences. Use the back of the handout if you need more space.

4. In the appropriate space on the handout, indicate where the animal fits in a food chain. Is it an herbivore or a carnivore?

5. Post your handout on the wall so that other students can learn about the animals you researched.

6. Continue writing questions and answers for other animals as time permits.

Animal Interview—*I wonder . . .*

Animal _____

1. Question:

   Answer:

2. Question:

   Answer:

3. Question:

   Answer:

4. Circle the true statement:

   This animal is an herbivore.   This animal is a carnivore.

(Some animals eat both plants and animals. They are called omnivores. If the animal is an omnivore, circle both statements.)

5. This animal belongs to the following food chain:

Center: Dinners & Diners

Multiple Intelligence: *Bodily-Kinesthetic*

Objective: Work together in a small group to pantomime a food chain.

Benchmarks:
Selects and organizes available materials that suggest scenery, props, and costumes. (The Arts: Theater 3, Level II)
Selects and creates elements of scenery, properties, lighting, and sound to signify environments, and costumes and makeup to suggest character. (The Arts: Theater 3, Level III)
Organizes rehearsals for improvised and scripted scenes. (The Arts: Theater 4, Level III)
Contributes to the overall effort of a group. (Life Skills: Working with Others 1, Levels I-IV)

Skill for Living: Vitality — being positive, energetic, and enthusiastic.

Materials:
- Information (books, magazines, etc.) about food chains including the book *Pass the Energy, Please!* Two other good books about food chains are *This is the Sea That Feeds Us* and *Tree in the Ancient Forest* (available from Dawn Publications).
- A wide variety of art supplies including construction paper, markers, glue, tape, etc.
- A wide variety of potential prop materials and costumes such as fabric, scarves, clothing, hats, fake fur, etc.

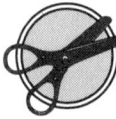
Teacher Preparation:
- Gather the arts and crafts and costume materials.
- Copy and laminate *Center Directions*.

Reflection Questions:
1. In what ways did your props, scenery, and costumes make the food chain interesting.?
2. How did you show that you were positive, energetic, and enthusiastic through your words and actions?

22

Center Directions:

Dinners & Diners

At this center you will:
Create a pantomime of a food chain.

Materials you should find at this center:
Information about food chains including the book *Pass the Energy, Please!*
A wide variety of art supplies including construction paper, markers, glue, tape, etc.
A wide variety of potential prop materials and costumes such as fabric, scarves, clothing, hats, fake fur, etc.

What you need to bring to this center:
Vitality — being positive, energetic, and enthusiastic.

Student Directions:

1. As a group, decide on a food chain that you will pantomime for the class. You may want to choose a food chain from one of the resources at this center including the book *Pass the Energy, Please*! You may also use one of the chains listed below.

2. Use the available materials to create props, scenery, and at least one costume piece for everyone.

3. Decide on the order of appearance and what actions and sounds each person will make. Rehearse your presentation by having each member of the food chain enter one at a time, briefly pose for the audience staying "in character." Once everyone is on-stage, act out the food chain through actions and sounds (you may use sound effects, but no speech).

4. After your rehearsal, give positive feedback to each other.

5. Your teacher will tell you when you will present your pantomime to the class. When you do, have your classmates guess the identity of each member of the food chain.

Other food chains that you can pantomime include:

Marine Food Chains

Sea plant – little fish – salmon – eagle

Sea plant – sea urchin – otter – orca

Plankton – shrimp – little fish – big fish – person (from *This is the Sea That Feeds Us*)

Land Food Chains

Tree root – truffle – mouse – owl (from *The Tree in the Ancient Forest*)

Grass – elephant – lion – vulture

Seed – quail – coyote – mountain lion

Center:

Create a Food Chain

Multiple Intelligence: *Interpersonal*

Objective:
Create an imaginary food chain on another planet that includes a plant, herbivore, at least one carnivore, and a decomposer.

Benchmarks:
Knows that some source of "energy" is needed for organisms to live and grow. (Science 8, Level II)

Knows that all animals depend on plants; some animals eat plants for food while others eat animals that eat the plants. (Science 8, Level II)

Knows that over the whole Earth, organisms are growing, dying, and decaying, and new organisms are being produced by the old ones. (Science 8, Level II)

Knows that animals and plants can be classified according to the function they serve in a food chain. (Science 4. Level III)

Displays effective interpersonal communication skills. (Life Skills : Working with Others 4, Level IV)

Skill for Living: Cooperation — working together and getting along with others.

Materials:
❏ Various arts and crafts supplies such as construction paper, colored markers, tissue paper, paint, glue, tape, pipe cleaners, cardboard, etc.

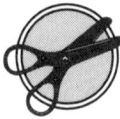

Teacher Preparation:
❏ Gather the art and craft materials.
❏ Copy and laminate *Center Directions*.

Reflection Questions:
1. In what ways did you cooperate with others while playing the game?
2. What words or actions did you use to show that you were trying to get along with others?
3. On what planet does your food chain exist?
4. How did the members of your food chain depend upon one another?

Center Directions:

Create a Food Chain

At this center you will:
Create an imaginary food chain from another planet that includes a plant, herbivore, carnivore, and decomposer.

Materials you should find at this center:
Various arts and crafts supplies such as construction paper, colored markers, tissue paper, paint, glue, tape, pipe cleaners, cardboard, etc.

What you need to bring to this center:
Paper and pencil.
Cooperation — working together and getting along with others.

Student Directions:

1. As a group, decide on a planet that will be the habitat of your food chain. You may choose a planet in our solar system or an imaginary planet.

2. Discuss how conditions on the planet (such as temperature range, amount of light, availability of water) effect the plants and animals that live there.

3. Brainstorm ideas about possible plants and animals that would live on the planet. Accept all ideas.

4. Choose one plant, herbivore, carnivore, and decomposer that would make up a single food chain.

5. Use the arts and crafts supplies to create the members of your food chain. Your group can work together in a variety of ways: everyone works on every part, each person creates one part, or two people work together on two parts. Decide as a group how you will work.

6. Your teacher will tell you how to display your food chain when you are finished.

25

Center:

Sounds Good

Multiple Intelligence: *Musical-Rhythmic*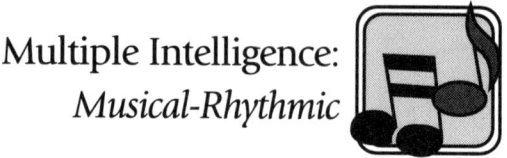

 ### *Objective:*
Create a read-aloud tape for *Pass the Energy, Please!* using appropriate sound effects.

 ### *Benchmarks:*
Applies the reading process and strategies to passages about general science. (Language Arts 11, Level II)

Demonstrates competence in speaking and listening as tools for learning. (Language Arts 11, Level II)

Improvises using a variety of sound sources, including traditional sounds (e.g., voices, instruments), nontraditional sounds (e.g., paper tearing, pencil tapping,), body sounds (e.g., hands clapping, fingers snapping), and sounds produced by electronic means. (The Arts: Music 3, Level II)

 ### *Skill for Living:* Creativity — approaching situations in fresh, new ways.

 ### *Materials:*
- Tape player — one per student group
- Blank tape — one per student group
- Quiet space to record
- Copy of the book *Pass the Energy, Please!* — one per student group
- Various noise makers such as running water, bird call, etc.
- Post It notes

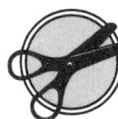 ### *Teacher Preparation:*
- Gather materials and place them at the center.
- Copy and laminate *Center Directions*.

 ### *Reflection Questions:*
1. What sounds were the most fun to make? To listen to?
2. Did your group follow the creative process? Did you brainstorm ideas and make changes and modifications in your sound effect ideas? Was this an effective way to create the tape? Why or why not?
3. What other books or stories do you know that could use sound effects?

Center Directions:

Sounds Good

At this center you will:
Create a read-aloud tape for *Pass the Energy, Please!* that uses interesting and appropriate sound effects.

Materials you should find at this center:
Tape player and a blank tape – one per student group
Quiet space to record
Copy of the book *Pass the Energy, Please!*
Various noise makers such as a bird call, bowl of water, etc.
Post It notes

What you need to bring to this center:
Pencil or pen
During the creation of the tape you may need to gather other items for making the sound effects.
Creativity — approaching situations in fresh, new ways.

Student Directions:

1. One person reads aloud the first page of *Pass the Energy, Please!* while the rest of the group listens.

2. After the page is read, brainstorm interesting sound effects that could go along with the text. Think about what items are available in the classroom that you could use to make the sound effect. Remember that in the creative process it is necessary to brainstorm a lot of ideas. **Don't rule out any ideas yet**.

3. Write all ideas on Post It notes and place them on the appropriate page in the book. Continue this process for the entire book. You may not have sound effects ideas for every page.

4. Collect any items you need to make the sound effects. You may not be able to find the items that you need for some of the sound effect ideas. Eliminate those ideas by removing the Post It notes.

5. Once you have everything you need, choose a narrator who will read the story and decide who will make each sound effect. Be sure to involve everyone in your group.

6. Rehearse for the taping by practicing all of the sound effects. Sound effects should fit into the rhythm and flow of the reading. Make changes and modifications as necessary.

7. Make an audio tape, listen to it, and make any refinements that you think will improve the tape.

8. Your teacher will tell you when you will share the finished tape with your class or another class.

Center:

Animal Cinquains

Multiple Intelligence: *Verbal-Linguistic*

Objective: Write cinquains about animals in food chains.

Benchmarks:
Demonstrates competence in expressive writing. (Language Arts 1, Level II)
Writes with a command of grammatical conventions. (Language Arts 3, Level II)

Skill for Living: Creativity — expressing oneself in fresh, new ways.

Materials:
- The book *Pass the Energy, Please!*
- *Animal Cinquain: Descriptive Poem* (Copy Master page 30) — two per student
- Various resources about animals including pictures.
- Colored pencils or marking pens.

Teacher Preparation:
- Make copies of *Animal Cinquain: Descriptive Poem.*
- Gather resources and colored pencils or pens.
- Copy and laminate *Center Directions.*

Reflection Questions:
1. Why did you choose the animals you wrote cinquains about?
2. Did you use any words that aren't part of your usual vocabulary?
3. How is writing poetry about an animal different than writing a report or answering questions?

Center Directions:

Animal Cinquains

At this center you will:
Write at least two cinquains about animals in a food chain.

Materials you should find at this center:
The book *Pass the Energy, Please!*
Copies of *Animal Cinquain: Descriptive Poem* — two per student
Various resources about animals including pictures.
Colored pencils or marking pens.

What you need to bring to this center:
Paper and pencil
Creativity — expressing oneself in fresh, new ways.

Student Directions:
Line 1: The subject that you are writing about (noun) — one word
Line 2: Words that describe your subject (adjectives) — two words
Line 3: Words that describe an action of the subject (end in -ing) — three words
Line 4: A phrase or sentence describing the subject — four words
Line 5: A word that means the same as the subject (synonym) — one word

Notice each line in the following example:

Panda
Masked, furry
Munching, sleeping, roaming
The panda looks cuddly.
Bear

1. Brainstorm several animals that you would like to write about. Use the resources and pictures at this center to give you ideas.

2. Choose an animal and write down several adjectives, action words, and any words that come to mind when you think of that animal. Write down any feelings that you have when you think about the animal.

3. Fill in the *Cinquain: Descriptive Poem* handout choosing your most descriptive words and ideas.

4. Illustrate your cinquain.

5. If time permits, write a cinquain for another animal.

Animal Cinquain: *Descriptive Poem*

_____
subject

_____   _____
adjective   adjective

_____ _____ _____
-ing action word -ing action word -ing action word

____ _____ _____ _____ .
sentence describing the subject

_____
synonym

Illustration

COPY MASTER

Center:

Paper Chains

Multiple Intelligence: *Visual-Spatial*

Objective: Create a bulletin board display using paper chains that represent food chains.

Benchmarks:
Knows ways in which the principles and subject matter of other disciplines taught in the school are interrelated with those of the arts. (The Arts 1, Level I)

Knows that all animals depend on plants; some animals eat plants for food while others eat animals that eat the plants. (Science 8, Level II)

Knows that all organisms, including the human species, are part of and depend on two main global food webs; one global food web starts with microscopic ocean plants and seaweed and includes the animals that feed on them and subsequent animals that feed on the plant-eating animals; the other global food web begins with land plants and includes the animals that feed on them. (Science 4, Level III)

Knows that major categories of living organisms are plants, which get their energy directly from sunlight, and animals, which consume energy-rich foods. (Science 4, Level III)

Skill for Living: Respect — showing regard for the worthiness of all life.

Materials:
- *Paper Chains — Plants* (Copy Master page 39) copied on green paper and cut apart – one copy per student.
- *Paper Chains — Herbivores* (Copy Master page 40) copied on blue paper and cut apart - one per student.
- *Paper Chains — Carnivores* (Copy Master page 41) copied on red paper and cut apart - one per student.
- Five shallow boxes (such as shoe boxes) labeled "Bamboo Forest" "Meadow Floor" "Arctic Ocean" "African Plain" and "Woodland"
- Glue or tape for students to share
- A copy of the book *Pass the Energy, Please!*
- Bulletin board with sun image in the center
- Push pins — two per student

Teacher Preparation:
- Cover a bulletin board with white paper and create a sun in the center.
- Copy handouts onto colored paper and cut apart.
- Label shallow boxes.
- Place the plant and animal strips by food chain in the appropriate boxes. For example, all of the bamboo and panda strips go in the box labeled "Bamboo Forest." All of the grass, gazelle, and cheetah strips go in the box labeled "African Plain."
- Copy and laminate *Center Directions*.
- After students make their paper chains, arrange the chains around the sun to create a mandala of food chains with the sun in the center.

Reflection Questions:
1. What pattern do you notice in the chains? With what color does each food chain begin?
2. What color link is always next to the green link? What type of animal does this color represent?
3. With what color paper do most of the food chains end?
4. What would happen to the food chains if there were no plants? What would happen to the food chains if there were no herbivores?
5. Why is it important to respect all living things?

Center Directions:

Paper Chains

At this center you will:
Put together paper chains that represent food chains. Your teacher will choose some of these paper chains to make a bulletin board display

Materials you should find at this center:
Five shallow boxes labeled "Bamboo Forest" "Meadow Floor" "Arctic Ocean" "African Plain" and "Woodland" filled with colored paper strips.
Glue or tape for students to share.
A copy of the book *Pass the Energy, Please!*

What you need to bring to this center:
Respect — showing regard for the worthiness of all life.

Student Directions:

1. Beginning with one of the boxes, find the strip of paper that has the name of the first link of the food chain. Make a loop by taping the ends of the strip together. Because you will want to be able to easily read the name on the paper, keep the name and picture of the plant on the outside of the loop.

2. Find the strip of paper with the name and picture of the animal that is the second link of the food chain. Make a loop with it connecting it to the first loop you made. Continue making a chain of loops until you have used all of the plants and animals in the food chain. You will find a complete food chain in each box; do not mix strips of paper among the boxes.

3. Continue making paper food chains from each box.

4. When finished, give all of the paper food chains to your teacher who will create a bulletin board display.

Paper Chains: *Plants*

Teacher Directions: Copy on green paper and cut apart into strips.

bamboo

seed

phytoplankton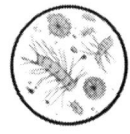

grass

goldenrod

Paper Chains: *Herbivores*

Teacher Directions: Copy on blue paper and cut apart into strips.

panda

mouse

zooplankton

gazelle

caterpillar

Paper Chains: *Carnivores*

Teacher Directions: Copy on red paper and cut apart into strips.

snake

anchovy

cheetah

spider

warbler

owl

seal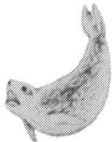

polar bear

weasel

red fox

COPY MASTER

Center:

Pyramid Power

Multiple Intelligence: *Visual-Spatial*

 ### Objective:
Create a poster illustrating the energy pyramid of plants, herbivores, and carnivores.

 ### Benchmarks:
Knows that all animals depend on plants; some animals eat plants for food while others eat animals that eat the plants. (Science 8, Level II)

Knows that major categories of living organisms are plants, which get their energy directly from sunlight, and animals, which consume energy-rich foods. (Science 4, Level III)

Knows that over the whole Earth, organisms are growing, dying, and decaying, and new organisms are being produced by the old ones. (Science 8, Level II)

Knows that all organisms, including the human species, are part of and depend on two main global food webs. (Science 4, Level III)

Knows that almost all food energy ultimately comes from the Sun as plants convert light into stored chemical energy. (Science 8, Level III)

Knows that all species ultimately depend on one another. (Science 7, Level III)

 ### Skill for Living: Respect — showing regard for the worthiness of all creatures.

 ### Materials:
- Various nature magazines such as *Ranger Rick, National Geographic, National* and *International Wildlife*
- Scissors – one per student
- Glue for students to share
- Plain white paper
- Colored pencils
- White poster board — one for each group that uses the center (See diagram on *Center Directions* handout)

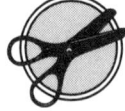 ### Teacher Preparation:
- Create a large sun with a pyramid inside it on a piece of poster board. Designate levels within the pyramid for plants, herbivores, and carnivores. Allow room outside of the pyramid for decomposers. (See diagram on *Center Directions* handout)
- Copy and laminate *Center Directions*

 ### Reflection Questions:
1. Why is the Sun at the center of the bulletin board?
2. Why are plants important to all life?
3. What type of animals are on the top of the food pyramid?
4. What is one of the ways that species depend on one another?
5. What is at least one reason why it is important to respect all living things? Give a specific example.

Center Directions:

Pyramid Power

At this center you will:
    Cut out pictures of plants, herbivores, carnivores, and decomposers to create a beautiful poster board.

Materials you should find at this center:
    Different kinds of magazines
    Scissors
    Glue
    Plain white paper
    Colored pencils

What you need to bring to this center:
    Pencil or pen
    Respect — showing regard for the worthiness of all creatures

Student Directions:

1. Read the following explanation of a pyramid of energy:

    The amount of energy available at each link in a food chain can be shown by using a pyramid.
    A small amount of the energy stored in plants (between five and 25 percent) passes into herbivores (plant eaters) as they feed. A similar percentage of the energy in herbivores then passes into carnivores (animal eaters).
    The result is a pyramid of energy with most of the energy concentrated in the plants at the bottom of food chains.
    Bacteria, fungi, scavengers, and other decomposers also consume energy and are eventually consumed by other organisms.

2. Using the magazines, cut out a picture of a plant, herbivore, carnivore. If you cannot find a picture in a magazine, you may draw your own picture on the white paper. Glue the picture to the poster board at the appropriate level. You may also find a picture of a decomposer which can be glued around the outside of the pyramid. Use enough pictures to completely fill the pyramid.

3. Label a separate piece of notebook paper with four columns: Plants, Herbivores, Carnivores, Decomposers and write in the names of the plants and animals that you put on the poster board.

Center: Weight and See

Multiple Intelligence: *Logical-Mathematical*

 *Objective:* Graph the weights of various animals.

 *Benchmarks:*
Understands that graphs can show how the values of one quantity are related to the values of another. (Math 6, Level II)
Constructs and interprets simple bar graphs. (Math 6, Level II)
Compares the differences between any two measurements. (Math 4, Level II)

 *Skill for Living:* Orderliness — demonstrating neatness and organization.

 *Materials:*
❑ *Weight and See — Bar Graphs* (Copy Master page 40) — one per student
❑ Variety of colored pencils — enough for two different colors per student

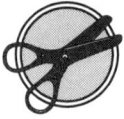 *Teacher Preparation:*
❑ Make copies of *Weight and See — Bar Graphs*.
❑ Copy and laminate *Center Directions* to be placed at the center location.

 *Reflection Questions:*
1. Which animal weighed the most? The least?
2. Were you surprised by how much or how little some animals weighed? Which ones?
3. Can you draw any conclusions about how much herbivores weigh compared to carnivores? What limits your ability to draw accurate conclusions?
4. How do graphs help to show the relationships between animals?
5. Were your graphs neat and easy to read?

Center Directions:

Weight and See

At this center you will:
Graph the weights of various animals.

Materials you should find at this center:
Copies of the handout *Weight and See — Bar Graphs* — one per student
Variety of colored pencils — enough for two different colors per student

What you need to bring to this center:
Orderliness — demonstrating neatness and organization.

Student Directions:

1. Fill in the two bar graphs using two different colored pencils: one color for herbivores and the other color for carnivores. Take care in creating the graphs to work neatly by coloring evenly within the lines.

2. Helpful Hint: Before beginning to make the graphs, use the correct colored pencil to lightly color over the word for each animal at the bottom of the graph. This will help you remember which color to use for each animal on the graph.

Animal Information: (animals pictured in *Pass the Energy, Please!*)

**Graph of Animals
That Weigh Less Than 5 Pounds**

Caterpillar — less than 1 ounce
Warbler — 1 ounce
Wood mouse — 1 ounce
Weasel — 4 ounces
Barn owl — 1 pound and 4 ounces
Rat snake — 1 pound and 8 ounces
Red fox — 3 pounds
Rabbit — 4 pounds
Turkey vulture — 4 pound and 8 ounces

**Graph of Animals
That Weigh More Than 50 Pounds**

Gazelle — 90 lbs.
Manatee — 100 lbs.
Cheetah — 120 lbs.
Whitetail deer — 150 lbs.
Panda — 220 lbs.
Harp seal — 400 lbs.
Polar Bear — 1000 lbs.
African elephant — 11,000 lbs.

Note: Weights vary greatly. The weights listed are averages for an adult male of the species.

Weight and See—Bar Graphs

Animals that Weigh Less Than 5 Pounds

4 lbs., 8 oz.									
4 lbs.									
3 lbs., 8 oz.									
3 lbs.									
2 lbs., 8 oz.									
2 lbs.									
1 lbs., 8 oz.									
1 lbs.									
8 oz.									
0	caterpillar	mouse	warbler	weasel	barn owl	rat snake	red fox	rabbit	vulture

Animals that Weigh More Than 50 Pounds

1,000 lbs.							
900 lbs.							
800 lbs.							
700 lbs.							
600 lbs.							
500 lbs.							
400 lbs.							
300 lbs.							
200 lbs.							
100 lbs.							
0	gazelle	manatee	cheetah	deer	panda	seal	polar bear

How much bigger would the graph need to be to include an elephant?

Center: Creature Features

Multiple Intelligence: *Logical-Mathematical*

Objective:
Compare personal physical abilities with animals' physical abilities.
Accurately make measurements in both customary and metric units.

Benchmarks:
Knows that plants or animals have a great variety of body plans and internal structures that contribute to their being able to make or find food and reproduce. (Science 4, Level II)

Knows that living systems at all levels of organization demonstrate complementarity of structure and function. (Science 6, Level III)

Makes effective use of a ruler and meter stick for making measurements. (Math 4, Level II)

Compares the differences between any two measurements. (Math 4, Level II)

Constructs and interprets simple bar graphs; understands that graphs can show how the values of one quantity are related to the values of another. (Math 6, Level II)

Skill for Living: Respect — valuing all life

Materials:
- Copies of *Creature Features — Measurements* (Copy Master page 43) — one per student.
- Tape Measure (six foot) — one per student pair.
- Meter stick — one per student pair.
- Stop watch — one per student pair.
- Eye chart — teacher-created or from the school nurse.
- Butcher paper to be posted on the wall to measure heights of students.
- Graph paper — six sheets labeled with measurement categories. (See *Center Directions*)

Teacher Preparation:
- Make copies of *Creature Features — Measurements*.
- Create (or obtain from school nurse) and post eye chart. Place the eye chart in a location where students can stand across the room and move closer.
- Tape a piece of butcher paper to the wall for students to measure heights.
- Label sheets of graph paper with categories (such as Resting Pulse), draw an x and y axis. Label the x axis with student names and the y axis with the customary measurement that is to be used. Optional: Additional graphs with metric measurements and student names.
- Copy and laminate *Center Directions*.

Reflection Questions:
1. How did your class compare with the various animals? In what areas were you most similar to the animal? Most different?
2. How do the animals' characteristics help them to be successful within their food chain?
3. Do you have greater respect or appreciation for the animals with which you compared yourself?
4. What are some human physical abilities that you appreciate having?

Center Directions:

Creature Features

At this center you will:
    Work in pairs to make measurements in both customary and metric units.
    Graph the results.

Materials you should find at this center:
    Tape measure — one per student pair
    Meter stick — one per student pair
    Stop watch — one per student pair
    Eye chart posted on the wall
    Butcher paper posted on the wall to measure height
    Graphs to record your measurements
    Copies of *Creature Features — Measurements* — one per student

What you need to bring to this center:
    Pencil or pen
    Respect — valuing all life.

Student Directions:

1. Work with a partner to complete the following tasks that are described on *Creature Features — Measurements*. You do not need to do the tasks in the same order as they appear on the handout. Select tasks so you do not need to wait for others at the eye chart and height measurement area.

2. Measure your results in both customary and metric units (when appropriate) and record your results on the handout using the following categories and measurements:

    Resting Pulse in beats per minute
    Running Pulse in beats per minute
    Height in feet and inches
    Eyesight in feet and inches
    Wingspan in inches
    Hold Breath in seconds

3. Record your measurements on the appropriate graph.

Creature Features—Measurements

Animals have many features that help them get food and survive. You will compare some of your human features with those of several animals.

Resting Pulse
A rabbit freezes and sits perfectly still so that a predator will not see it. Sit perfectly still for 3 minutes. Immediately take your pulse.

How to Take Your Pulse
1. Find your pulse at either your wrist or your neck by touching the artery lightly with two or three fingers.
2. Your partner will time you for six seconds while you count your pulse.
3. Add a zero to the number you got and that is your pulse in beats per minute.

My resting pulse is _____

Running Pulse
A cheetah is the fastest animal on Earth and can run as fast as 60 to 70 miles per hour in a short burst of speed. It can only run this fast for about 20 seconds or 300 yards. Run in place at your top speed for 20 seconds while your partner times you. Take your pulse and record it.

My running pulse is _____.

Height
A giraffe averages 18 feet tall and relies on its long neck and legs to help it reach acacia leaves that are its primary food source. Have your partner measure how tall you are. Record your height on the paper on the wall and on this sheet.

My height is (feet and inches) _____

My height is

(meters and centimeters) _____

Eyesight
Vultures have excellent vision and can see a three-foot carcass (dead animal) from four miles away! Stand across the room from the eye chart and try to read the bottom line. If you cannot read it, step forward a little at a time until you can accurately read all of the letters. Have your partner check you for accuracy. Measure the distance.

I could read the chart at

(feet and inches) _____

I could read the chart at

(meters and centimeters) _____.

Wingspan
An barn owl's wingspan is 45 inches. Hold your arms straight out from your sides and have your partner measure the distance from the fingertips of your left hand to the fingertips of your right hand.

My wingspan is

(inches) _____.

My wingspan is

(meters and centimeters) _____.

Hold Your Breath
A seal holds its breath for 20 to 30 minutes under water. Check to see how long you can hold your breath. Practice one time. Then have your partner time you using the stop watch. Record your time.

I can hold my breath for _____

Note: The resting and running pulse activities are adapted from *TOPS Science*.

Teacher Background Information

Energy Transfer

A small amount of the energy stored in plants, between five and 25 percent, passes into herbivores as they feed, and a similarly small percentage of the energy in herbivores then passes into carnivores. The result is a pyramid of energy, with most energy concentrated in the photosynthetic organisms at the bottom of food chains and less energy at each higher trophic level. Some of the remaining energy does not pass directly into the plant-herbivore-carnivore food chain, instead it is diverted into the detritus food chain. Bacteria, fungi, scavengers, carrion eaters and other decomposers that consume detritus are all eventually consumed by other organisms.

Energy is lost in several ways as it flows along these pathways of consumption. Most plant tissue is uneaten by herbivores, and this stored energy is therefore lost to the plant-herbivore-carnivore food chain. In terrestrial communities less than 10 percent of plant tissue is actually consumed by herbivores. The rest falls into the detritus pathway, although the detritivores consume only some of this decaying tissue. Oil and coal deposits are major repositories of this unused plant energy and have accumulated over long periods of geologic time.

Herbivores' bodies can't digest and use all of the plant material that they consume. Herbivores assimilate between 15 and 80 percent of the plant material they ingest, depending on their physiology and the part of the plant that they eat. For example, herbivores that eat seeds and young vegetation high in energy have the highest assimilation efficiencies, those that eat older leaves have intermediate efficiencies, and those that feed on decaying wood have very low efficiencies. Carnivores generally have higher assimilation efficiencies than herbivores, often between 60 and 90 percent, because their food is more easily digested.

Habitat Destruction

> Ecosystems will only survive
> If balanced food chains keep species alive.
> Too much of this, too little of that,
> Threatened a healthy habitat.
> We endanger the creatures by taking their space —
> They can't make their homes in the natural lace.
> Their food sources dwindle, they die of starvation,
> And food chains are weakened, a bad situation.

Habitat destruction is a serious threat to the plants and animals of all ecosystems. Pollution, development, global warming, acid rain, over-harvesting, and the introduction of non-native species are some of the causes of habitat destruction. A suggested follow-up unit is to teach students about habitats around the world and how to keep them healthy.

Science Terms and Definitions

Pass the Energy, Please! introduces many science terms and concepts through delightful poetry.

photosynthesis — the process by which plants use sunlight to make carbohydrates

chlorophyll — the green part of plants that enables photosynthesis to happen

nocturnal — active at night

osmosis — the movement of water into a plant's roots from the soil

herbivore — plant-eater

carnivore — meat-eater

ecosystem — plants and animals in their environment

predator — an animal that lives by killing other animals for food

prey — an animal that is killed for food

zooplankton — a microscopic sea animal

phytoplankton — a microscopic sea plant

consumer — an animal that eats a plant or animal in its environment

producer — a plant or animal that is available as a source of food

There are many ways that a teacher can make the most of using the new vocabulary. For example:

Divide the class into small groups of three to five students each. Give each group a copy of the book *Pass the Energy, Please!* and have them compile a list of new vocabulary words. Then have them pass their list to another group who looks up the words and writes out a definition.

Have students create Crossword Puzzles or Word Search Puzzles to be solved by other students.

Play a game of "Pictionary" using the new science vocabulary words.

Divide the class in half. Give half of the words to one group and the other half to the other group. Give each group a dictionary. Allow fifteen minutes for each group to figure out actions that will define the words. For example, everyone acting as though they were sleeping could be the action for the word nocturnal. Allow students to use any props that are readily available.

Multiple Intelligences Subcapacities

Bodily-Kinesthetic
- Sense of Timing
- Direct Involvement
- Concrete Experiences
- Grace and Precision
- Physical Performance
- Motor Skills
- Dexterity and Balance
- Expresses with Body
- Do, Touch, Act
- Touches and Talks
- Energetic

Intrapersonal
- Asks Why
- Strong-Willed
- Self-Reflective
- Marches to a Different Drummer
- Self-Actualizer
- Intuitive
- Conscious Consciousness
- Introspective
- Self-Directed
- Independent
- Accurate Model of Self
- Ethical System

(Not necessarily introverted)

Musical-Rhythmic
- Collects Music, Records, Tapes, CDs
- Sings and Plays
- Music Vocabulary
- Creative
- Remembers Melodies
- Hums and Whistles
- Rhythmic
- Pitch Sensitivity
- Drawn to Music
- Responds to Sound
- Emotional and Aesthetic
- Recognizes Variations in Music

Verbal-Linguistic
- Highly Auditory
- A Reader
- Processes Through Listening
- A Storyteller
- Understands Diverse Vocabulary
- A Good Speller
- A Wordsmith
- Etymology Trivia
- Awakened by Words
- Loquacious
- Writes Endings
- "Tape-Recorder Memory"

Interpersonal
- Socializer
- Interactive
- Mediator
- Active Listener
- Considers Consequences
- Anticipates Behaviors
- Adapts Behaviors
- Opinion Influencer
- Cooperative Team Player
- Communicator
- Knows Where Others are Coming From
- Empathizer

Logical-Mathematical
- Makes and Uses Patterns
- Discerns Relationships
- Reasons Logically
- Devises Experiments
- Thinks Inductively
- Hypothesizes
- Uses Abstract Symbols
- Easily Draws Conclusions
- Inventive
- Likes Challenges
- Makes Observations
- Problem Solves

Naturalist
- Holistic Thinker
- Sees Relationships
- Connects Capabilities
- Recognizes Specimens
- Values the Unusual
- Aware of Species: Flora, Fauna
- Classifies Species
- Categorizes Organisms

Visual-Spatial
- Internal Imagery
- Physical Creator
- 3-D Imagery
- Perceives Patterns
- Abstract Designs
- Uses Visual Representations
- Astute Observer
- Enjoys Mazes and Puzzles
- Spatial Navigator
- Image Creator
- Photographic Memory
- External Perceiver

How to Teach to the Eight Intelligences

Bodily-Kinesthetic
Use touching, feeling, movement, drama, mime, improvisation, dance, competitive and noncompetitive sports, physical awareness exercises, "hands-on" activities, crafts, kinesthetic imagery, clay, cooking, gardening and other messy activities, manipulating materials of all kinds, acting out new concepts, permission to squirm and fidget, jumping, running, tapping and turning, body language, hand signals, tactile activities, facial expressions, physical relaxation exercises.

Interpersonal
Use cooperative learning, group activities of all kinds, social games, simulations, interpersonal sensitivity activities, conflict mediation, peer teaching, group discussions and problem-solving sessions. community involvement, apprenticeships, academic clubs, noncompetitive learning groups, interactive software, frequent parties or social gatherings.

Intrapersonal
Use independent study, self-paced instruction, individualized projects and games, private spaces, time for introspection, patience, interest centers, biographies, autobiographical exercises, options for assignments, choices for subjects to be studied, self-initiated activities, self-correcting materials, programmed instruction that self-teaches, exposure to inspirational/motivational curricula, journal-keeping activities, goal-setting exercises.

Logical-Mathematical
Use calculators, statistical charts, mathematical problems on the board, scientific demonstrations, critical-thinking activities, linear outlining, logical problem-solving exercises, brain teasers, logic games (chess, Go, etc.), computer programming languages, science experiments, mathematical manipulatives, mental calculation activities, logical/sequential presentation of subject matter, use of probing questions, science fiction scenarios.

Musical-Rhythmic
Use singing, humming, whistling; playing recorded music from records, cassettes, or CDs; group playing with percussion instruments; student playing of individual instruments, playing live music on the piano, guitar, etc.; group singing; environmental sound recordings; listening to noises in background; background music while studying; linking old tunes with new concepts; creating new music or old concepts; listening to inner musical images.

Naturalist
Use relationships among systems or species; collections and real objects for the purpose of classification and building taxonomies; intuitive concepts and relationships; classification activities; relationships such as patterns, order, and compare and contrast sets of groups; collections that can be expanded or rearranged; mind mapping to show how taxonomies and classification systems are interrelated; connections to real life and science issues; connection between known classification systems and new concepts.

Verbal-Linguistic
Use lectures, large and small group discussions, books, worksheets, manuals, texts, writing activities, words on the chalkboard or overhead projector, word games, sharing time, student speeches, storytelling, "talking" books and cassettes, extemporaneous speaking, oratory, debate, dramatic interpretation, choral reading, individualized reading, reading to the class, memorizing linguistic passages and facts, tape recording, "word" rubber stamps and stickers, printing presses, duplicating machines, letter stencils, label markers, typewriters, word processors.

Visual-Spatial
Use charts, graphs, diagrams, maps, graphic organizers, mind maps, photographs, videotapes, slides, movies, puzzles, mazes, construction kits (Lego®, clay'n straw, etc.), visualization exercises, art activities, imaginative storytelling, metaphor, creative daydreaming, mechanical reasoning puzzles, drawing images on the board, rearrangement of the room, visual thinning exercises, computer graphics software, visual patterns, optical illusions, cameras, telescopes, microscopes and binoculars; doodling, "picture" rubber stamps and stickers, visual awareness exercises.

Resources

Books for Teachers

Purposeful Learning Through Multiple Intelligences by Miriam Georg, Performance Learning Systems, 1997

Multiple Intelligences in the Classroom by Thomas Armstrong, ASCD, 1994

Multiple Intelligences: The Complete MI Book by Dr. Spencer Kagan & Miguel Kagan, Kagan Cooperative Learning, 1998

Celebrating Multiple Intelligences: Teaching for Success by the Faculty of the New City School, 1994

Multiple Assessments for Multiple Intelligences by James Bellanca, Carolyn Chapman, Elizabeth Swartz, IRI/Skyline Publishing, 1994

Your Child's Growing Mind: A Practical Guide to Brain Development and Learning from Birth to Adolescence by Jane M. Healy, Doubleday, 1987

Smart Moves: Why Learning Is Not All In Your Head by Carla Hannaford, Great Ocean Publishers, 1995

Brain Gym by Paul and Gail Dennison, 1986

Super Teaching by Eric Jensen, Turning Point Publishing, 1995

Tribes by Jeanne Gibbs, Center Source Publications, 1987

TOPS Learning Systems by Ron Marsten, Canby, Oregon

Educating for Character by Thomas Lickona, Bantam Books, 1991

Integrated Thematic Instruction: The Model by Susan Kovalik, 1993

Frames of Mind: Theory of Multiple Intelligences by Howard Gardner, Basic Books, Inc., 1983

Helpful Catalogs for Teacher Materials

Performance Learning Systems, 224 Church St., Nevada City, CA 95959, Phone: 800-255-8412

Zephyr Press, 3316 N. Chapel Ave., Tucson, Arizona 857728-6006, Phone: 800-232-2187

Synergistics®, P.O. 84, Windsor Hill, CT 06028-0084, Phone: 260-291-9499

Related Resources from Dawn Publications

This is the Sea that Feeds Us by Bob Baldwin. In cumulative verse, this book introduces the marine food web, from plankton to a thankful human family. Ages 4-12. 32pp.

Tree in the Ancient Forest by Carol Reed Jones. In cumulative verse, this book explores the interdependence of forest flora and fauna that surround one ancient fir tree. Ages 4-10. 32pp.

A Drop Around the World by Barbara McKinney. World-wide habitats and ecosystems are explored by a drop of water. Ages 5-12. 32pp. Teacher's guide available, 48pp.

Dandelion Seed by Joseph Anthony. The adventures and life cycle of a single dandelion seed illustrate seed dispersal and become a metaphor for growth, courage, challenge, and acceptance.

Dawn Publications is dedicated to inspiring in children a deeper understanding and appreciation for all life on Earth. To order, or for a copy of our catalog, please call 800-545-7475. Please also visit our web site at www.dawnpub.com.